GW00648300

Giftbooks in this "Words for Life" series:

Words on Hope	Words on Joy
Words of Courage	Words on Kindness
Words of Wisdom	Words on Love and Caring
Words on Compassion	Words on Solitude and Silence
Words on Beauty	Words on Strength and Perseverance
Words on Calm	Words on a Simple Life

Published simultaneously in 1998 by Exley Publications Ltd. in Great Britain, and Exley Publications LLC in the USA.
Copyright © Helen Exley 1998
The moral right of the author has been asserted.

12 11 10 9 8 7 6 5 4 3 2 1

Edited and pictures selected by Helen Exley
ISBN 1-86187-046-9

Printed in Hungary.

Exley Publications Ltd, 16 Chalk Hill, Watford, Herts WD1 4BN, UK.
Exley Publications LLC, 232 Madison Avenue, Suite 1206, NY 10016, USA.

Words on a Simple Life

A HELEN EXLEY
GIFTBOOK

NEW YORK • WATFORD, UK

*H*ow simple and frugal
a thing is happiness: a glass
of wine, a roast chestnut,
a wretched little brazier,
the sound of the sea....
All that is required to feel
that here and now is
happiness is a simple,
frugal heart.

NIKOS KAZANTZAKIS
(1885-1957)

*P*ROPERTY IS NOT ESSENTIAL.
BUT HAPPINESS,
A LOVE OF BEAUTY,
FRIENDSHIP BETWEEN ALL
PEOPLES AND INDIVIDUALS,
IS LIFE ITSELF.

LAURIE STOCKWELL

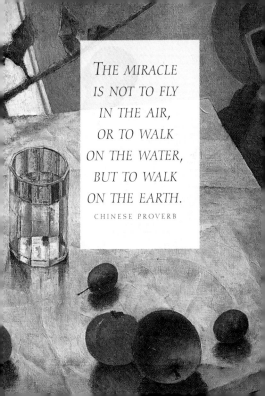

THE MIRACLE
IS NOT TO FLY
IN THE AIR,
OR TO WALK
ON THE WATER,
BUT TO WALK
ON THE EARTH.

CHINESE PROVERB

*THERE IS GREAT
HAPPINESS
IN NOT WANTING,
IN NOT BEING
SOMETHING,
IN NOT GOING
SOMEWHERE.*

J. KRISHNAMURTI
(1895-1986)

I think that a person who is attached to riches, who lives with the worry of riches, is actually very poor. If this person puts his money at the service of others, then he is rich, very rich.

MOTHER TERESA
(1910-1997)

To be content with what we possess is the greatest and most secure of riches.

MARCUS TULLIUS CICERO
(106-43 BC)

Let your boat of life
be light, packed only with
what you need – a homely
home and simple pleasures,
one or two friends worth
the name, someone to love
and to love you, a cat,
a dog, enough to eat and
enough to wear....

JEROME K. JEROME
(1859-1927)

*He is happiest, be he king
or peasant, who finds peace
in his home.*

JOHANN WOLFGANG VON
GOETHE
(1749-1832)

I believe we would be happier to have a personal revolution in our individual lives and go back to simpler living and more direct thinking. It is the simple things of life that make living worth while, the sweet fundamental things such as love and duty, work and rest and living close to nature.

LAURA INGALLS WILDER

*T*o be without
some of the things
you want is an
indispensable part
of happiness.

BERTRAND RUSSELL
(1872-1970)

*O*ne cannot collect
all the beautiful shells
on the beach.
One can collect
only a few,
and they are more
beautiful if they
are few.

ANNE MORROW LINDBERGH,
FROM "GIFT FROM THE SEA"

Though the search for simplicity is, at any time, a difficult journey through a wilderness, we can learn from guides ancient and modern. People who despair because their calendars are so crowded and their duties demanding have to put a premium on simplicity. Some find a way by clearing a special room and a certain hour in which they can strip away what matters finally in their lives....

MARTIN MARTY

Go confidently
in the direction of your
dreams! Live the life
you've imagined.
As you simplify your life,
the laws of the universe
will be simpler; solitude
will not be solitude,
poverty will not be
poverty, nor weakness
weakness.

HENRY DAVID THOREAU
(1817-1862)

*T*HE SECRET
OF CONTENTMENT
IS KNOWING
HOW TO ENJOY
WHAT YOU HAVE,
AND TO BE ABLE
TO LOSE ALL DESIRE
FOR THINGS BEYOND
YOUR REACH.

LIN YUTANG
(1895-1976)

*Poor and content is rich,
and rich enough.*

WILLIAM SHAKESPEARE
(1564-1616)

*He or she who knows
that enough is enough will
always have enough.*

LAO-TZU
(6TH CENTURY B.C.)

It becomes necessary
to learn how to clear the
mind of all clouds, to free it
of all useless ballast and
debris by dismissing the
burden of too much concern
with material things.

INDRA DEVI

*There are so few empty pages
in my engagement pad, or empty
hours in the day, or empty rooms
in my life in which to stand alone
and find myself.
Too many activities, and people,
and things, and interesting people.
For it is not merely the trivial
which clutters our lives but the
important as well. We can have
a surfeit of treasures....*

ANNE MORROW LINDBERGH,
FROM "GIFT FROM THE SEA"

Sooner or later we all discover that the important moments in life are not the advertised ones, not the birthdays, the graduations, the weddings, not the great goals achieved. The real milestones are less prepossessing. They come to the door of memory unannounced, stray dogs that amble in, sniff around a bit, and simply never leave. Our lives are measured by these.

SUSAN B. ANTHONY

my earliest emotions
are bound to the earth
and to the labors of the
fields. I find in the land
a profound suggestion of
poverty and I love poverty
above all other things;
not sordid and famished
poverty but poverty that
is blessed – simple,
humble, like brown bread.

FREDERICO GARCIA LORCA
(1898-1936)

Nothing will content those who are not content with a little.

GREEK PROVERB

A bag of apples, a pot of homemade jam, a scribbled note, a bunch of golden flowers, a coloured pebble, a box of seedlings, an empty scent bottle for the children.... Who needs diamonds and van-delivered bouquets?

PAM BROWN, b.1928

LESS IS MORE.

ROBERT BROWNING
(1812-1889)

I HOPE YOU FIND JOY
IN THE GREAT THINGS OF LIFE —
BUT ALSO
IN THE LITTLE THINGS.

A FLOWER, A SONG,
A BUTTERFLY
ON YOUR HAND.

ELLEN LEVINE

I have learned to have
very modest goals
for society and myself;
things like clean air,
green grass, children with
bright eyes, not being
pushed around,
useful work that suits
one's abilities, plain
tasty food, and occasional
satisfying nookie.

PAUL GOODMAN

May we never let
the things we can't have,
or don't have, or shouldn't
have, spoil our enjoyment
of the things we do have
and can have. As we value
our happiness let us not
forget it, for one of the
greatest lessons in life is
learning to be happy
without the things
we cannot or should
not have.

RICHARD L. EVANS

IF YOU DON'T ENJOY
WHAT YOU HAVE, HOW COULD
YOU BE HAPPIER WITH MORE?

AUTHOR UNKNOWN

A small house
will hold
as much happiness
as a big one.

Gentleness is everywhere in daily life, a sign that faith rules through ordinary things: through cooking and small talk, through storytelling, making love, fishing, tending animals and sweetcorn and flowers, through sports, music and books, raising kids – all the places where the gravy soaks in and grace shines through. Even in a time of elephantine vanity and greed, one never has to look far to see the campfires of gentle people.

GARRISON KEILLOR, b.1942

Days tumbled on days, I was
in my overalls, didn't comb
my hair, didn't shave much,
consorted only with dogs and cats,
I was living the happy life of
childhood again.... I was as nutty
as a fruitcake and happier.
Sunday afteroon, then, I'd go
to my woods with the dogs
and sit and put out my hands
palms up and accept handfuls
of sun boiling over the palms.

JACK KEROUAC (1922-1969),
FROM "THE DHARMA BUMS"

WE ARE INVOLVED
IN A LIFE THAT PASSES
UNDERSTANDING AND OUR
HIGHEST BUSINESS IS
OUR DAILY LIFE.

JOHN CAGE
(1912-1992), FROM
"WHERE ARE WE GOING
AND WHAT ARE WE DOING?"

Yes, to become simple
and live simply, not only
within yourself but also in
your everyday dealings.
Don't make ripples all
around you, don't try so
hard to be interesting,
keep your distance,
be honest, fight the desire
to be thought fascinating
by the outside world.

ETTY HILLESUM

One day there springs up
the desire for money
and for all that money can
provide – the superfluous,
luxury in eating, luxury
in dressing, trifles.
Needs increase because one
thing calls for another.
The result is uncontrollable
dissatisfation. If you have
to go shopping, pick up the
simplest things.
We have to be happy

with our poverty.
Let us not be driven
by our small egotisms.

MOTHER TERESA
(1910-1997)

Money is not something
to go mad about, and throw
your hat in the air for.
*Money is for food and clothes
and comfort, and a visit to the
pictures. Money is to make
happy the lives of children.
Money is for security, and for
dreams, and for hopes, and for
purposes. Money is for buying
the fruits of the earth, of the
land where you were born.*

ALAN PATON,
FROM "CRY, THE BELOVED COUNTRY"

YOU CAN'T
HAVE EVERYTHING.
WHERE WOULD YOU
PUT IT?

ANN LANDERS

*The tipi is much
better to live in;
always clean,
warm in winter,
cool in summer;
easy to move.
The white man
builds big house,
cost much money,
like big cage,
shut out sun,
can never move;
always sick.*

CHIEF FLYING HAWK
(1852-1931)

*D*o nondoing, strive for
nonstriving, savour
the flavourless, regard
the small as important,
make much of little,
repay enmity with virtue;
plan for difficulty when
it is still easy, do the great
while it is still small.

LAO-TZU
(6TH CENTURY B.C.)

Countries like ours are full of people who have all of the material comforts they desire, yet lead lives of quiet (and at times noisy) desperation, understanding nothing but the fact that there is a hole inside them and that however much food and drink they pour into it, however many motorcars and television sets they stuff it with, however many well-balanced children and

*loyal friends they parade
around the edges of it...
it aches!*

BERNARD LEVIN

my life...
I began to realize, lacks
this quality of significance
and therefore of beauty,
because there is so little
empty space. The space
is scribbled on; the time
has been filled.

ANNE MORROW LINDBERGH,
FROM "GIFT FROM THE SEA"

Simplify. Stop bothering
with the non-essentials.
Having devoted my life
to my work so far,
I should reap the harvest
and learn how to live
the rest of it properly.
It's time now for trees
and grass and
growing things.

AUTHOR UNKNOWN

*T*o awaken each morning with
a smile brightening my face;
to greet the day with reverence
for the opportunities it contains;
to approach my work with
a clean mind; to hold ever before
me, even in the doing of little
things, the ultimate purpose
toward which I am working;
to meet men and women
with laughter on my lips
and love in my heart; to be
gentle, kind, and courteous
through all the hours;

to approach the night with
weariness that ever woos sleep
and the joy that comes
from work well done – this is
how I desire to waste wisely
my days.

THOMAS DEKKER
(c.1570-c.1641)

I asked for riches that I
might be happy;
I was given poverty that I
might be wise.

I asked for all things that I
might enjoy life;
I was given life that I
might enjoy all things.

I was given nothing that I
asked for;
But everything that I had
hoped for.

AUTHOR UNKNOWN

Acknowledgements: The publishers are grateful for permission to reproduce copyright material. Whilst every reasonable effort has been made to trace copyright holders, the publishers would be pleased to hear from any not here acknowledged. JACK KEROUAC: From *Dharma Bums,* published by Penguin Books. © 1958 Jack Kerouac, renewed 1986 Stella Kerouac and Jan Kerouac. BERNARD LEVIN: From The Times, 1968. ANNE MORROW LINDBERGH: Extracts from *Gift From The Sea,* © Anne Morrow Lindbergh 1955, 1975, renewed 1983 by Anne Morrow Lindbergh. Published by Pantheon Books and Random House UK Ltd. MARTIN MARTY: From *In Search of Simplicity* in The Readers Digest, April 1980. ALAN PATON: From *Cry, The Beloved Country,* published by Scribner. MOTHER TERESA: From *A Life For God,* © 1995 Servant Books. *Heart of Joy* by Mother Teresa, first published by Servant Books © 1995 Jose Luis Gonzalez-Balado.

Picture credits: Exley Publications would like to thank the following organizations and individuals for permission to reproduce their pictures. Whilst every reasonable effort has been made to trace copyright holders, the publishers would be pleased to hear from any not here acknowledged. AISA, Art Resource (AR), Artworks, Bridgeman Art Library (BAL), Fine Art Photographic Library (FAP), Giraudon, Snark International, SuperStock (SS). Cover and title page: Yun Shouping, *Album of Flower Paintings,* SS; page 7: Paul Cézanne, *L'Estanque,* AISA; page 8: Giovanni Battista Spinelli, *The Shower Of Gold,* Scala; pages 10/11: Kuzma Petrov-Vodkin, *Still Life,* AR; pages 12/13: © 1998 Julian Novorol,

November Moon, BAL; pages 14/15: Filonou, *Portrait of the Artist's Sister,* Giraudon; pages 16/17: © 1998 Kyffin Williams, *Thatched Cottages,* BAL; page 18: Alexander Mann, *Women Sifting Couscous,* SS; page 21: Vincent Van Gogh, *Sunflowers;* page 23: © 1998 Margaret Preston, *Rock Lily,* BAL; page 24: © 1998 Anna Ancher, *Bouquet of Clematis,* Snark International; page 26: © 1998 Charles Neal, *The Rose Standard,* SS; page 29: © 1998 Dan Brown, Artworks; page 31: © 1998 Charles Neal, *South Cerney Allotment,* SS; page 32: Odilon Redon, *Geraniums and Wild Flowers,* Giraudon; page 35: © 1998 Sir George Clausen, *In The Orchard,* BAL; page 36: © 1998 Fernando C. Amorsolo, *Cooking Under the Mango Tree;* page 39: Paul Cézanne, *Still Life;* pages 40/41: © 1998 Diana Armfield, *Wild Flowers and Grasses,* BAL; page 42: ©1998 Martha Walter, *Garden Still Life,* SS; page 45: Coquelin, *Still Life,* Giraudon; pages 46/47: © 1998 Claude Strachan, *Mother and Children,* BAL; page 49: Michael Peter Ancher, *Children and Young Girls,* BAL; pages 50/51: John Hollis Kaufmann, *Zinnias,* SS; page 53: © 1998 Diego Rivera, *Tejedora,* SS; page 55: © 1998 Timothy Easton, *May Petals on the Moat Edge;* page 57: James Hayllar, *Chacun à son goût,* FAP; page 58: Paul Gauguin, *Still Life with Fruit;* pages 60/61: Hugh L. Norris, *A Herbaceous Border,* BAL; pages 62/63: Fernand Khnopff, Fosset; *Still Life,* BAL; page 65: Claude Monet, *Yellow Irises and Pink Cloud;* pages 66/67: A. Herrman-Allyan, *Damsons,* FAP; page 68: Spencer Frederick Gore, *View from a Window,* BAL; page 70: Charles Angrand, *In The Garden,* BAL; page 73: Claude Monet, *Azaleas;* page 74: © 1998 Martha Walter, *Purple and White,* SS.